HOW TO MAKE CURTAINS

Measuring and Making the Perfect Window
Coverings for Every Room in Your Home

Rebecca Yaker

Storey

The mission of Storey Publishing is to serve our customers by publishing practical information that encourages personal independence in harmony with the environment.

Edited by Nancy D. Wood and Melinda A. Slaving
Series design by Alethea Morrison
Art direction by Jeff Stiefel and Michaela Jebb
Text production by Theresa Wiscovitch
Indexed by Christine R. Lindemer, Boston Road Communications

Cover illustration by © Ashley Le Quere
Interior illustrations by Allegra Lockstadt

Storey Publishing
210 MASS MoCA Way
North Adams, MA 01247
www.storey.com

Printed in the United States by McNaughton & Gunn, Inc.
10 9 8 7 6 5 4 3 2 1

LIBRARY OF CONGRESS CATALOGING-IN-PUBLICATION DATA

Yaker, Rebecca.
  How to make curtains : measuring and making the perfect window coverings for every room in your home / Rebecca Yaker.
    pages cm
  ISBN 978-1-61212-539-8 (pbk. : alk. paper)
  ISBN 978-1-61212-540-4 (ebook) 1. Draperies. I. Title.
TT390.Y35 2015
746.9'4—dc23
                                    2015009440

CONTENTS

CHAPTER ONE

WINDOW DRESSINGS

Windows are natural focal points. They come in all shapes and sizes, and chances are you have some in every room in your home. You may sit in front of a window to bask in the warm sunlight during the cooler months, or open your windows wide to welcome fresh breezes during the warmer months. Over the years, moving from apartment to apartment and finally to a home of my own, I came to realize that one of the key elements for making my house truly feel like a home was the addition of window coverings. It's amazing how such a simple addition can perfectly finish a space.

ANATOMY OF A WINDOW

Look closely at your windows. Notice how they open (in or out, such as an awning type window; up or down, such as a single- or double-hung window), or if they can't be opened at all (such as a picture or fixed window). Is the woodwork surrounding the window beautiful and something you wish to showcase, or unsightly and something you'd prefer to conceal? Is the window in a high-traffic location or above a piece of furniture or radiator? These are just a few of the considerations I will cover throughout this book to assist you in designing and making the perfect custom window covering to transform your space and reflect your personal style.

Window types abound — big, little, square, rectangular, round, and so many more. Here are the five most common types of windows, each representing the perfect canvas for new window coverings.

Fixed or picture windows. This type of window cannot be opened. It may have a decorative element, such as beveled-, leaded-, or stained-glass panels, but the primary function of this type of window is to allow light into a space.

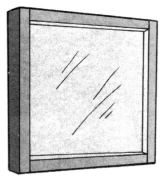

fixed or picture window

Single- or double-hung windows. Sometimes called a sash window, a single-hung window has a bottom window that slides up to open, while the top window is fixed. In a double-hung window, both upper and lower windows are moveable so the window can open either bottom up or top down. These windows are probably the most common and the easiest to design curtains for because of their regular, rectangular shape. Also, the way in which the window opens does not limit curtain styling.

single-hung   double-hung

Sliding or glider windows. Similar to single- and double-hung windows, these windows also slide open, but instead of top to bottom, they slide left to right (or vice versa). This window type is most commonly used in very wide spaces. For example, you can install one wide sliding window in a space that would typically require two sash windows installed side-by-side. This helps create the illusion of a larger space while allowing more natural light and view.

sliding window

Casement or awning windows. These windows are hinged vertically along the sides and typically open using a hand crank. They may open in or out, depending on the window style you have. Awning windows are similar to casement, except that their hinges are along either the top or bottom edges of the window. Curtain options can be a little more limited for casement and awning windows, especially if the windows open into the room.

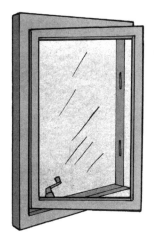

casement window

awning window

Bay windows. These windows are signified by an arrangement of three or more windows (the actual windows making up the configuration may be any or all of the four styles shown on pages 2–5), creating an angled alcove opening. The perfect window covering for your bay windows might be a separate covering for each window, following the contour of the recessed bay space. Another option would be to hang a rod outside the recess so that curtain panels conceal the entire bay window when closed. Some bay windows may be accompanied by window seats, which will affect the finished dimensions of the curtains.

Window Vocabulary

These are the individual components that make up a window.

1. **Pane.** The glass that is held in place by the sash.

2. **Sash.** The window frame that surrounds the panes of glass. The sash may be fixed (as is the case of fixed windows) or operable (as in single- or double-hung windows, shown in the illustration).

3. **Jamb.** The vertical side pieces of a window frame that surround and support the sash.

4. **Head.** The main horizontal top piece of a window frame that helps support the sash.

5. **Molding.** The decorative wood that surrounds and frames the window and finishes the space.

6. **Frame.** The combination of the head, jambs, and sill that forms a precise opening in which a window sash fits.

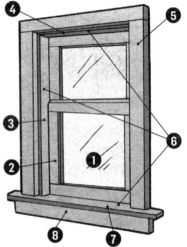

7. **Sill.** The horizontal shelf that sits below the window sash and above the apron.

8. **Apron.** A decorative piece of molding beneath the windowsill.

Although the five types of windows vary in their opening style, they are all suitable for curtains. You will need to take style into consideration so the window covering does not interfere with the way in which the window opens.

Once you determine your window type, take a look at the area surrounding it. Pay close attention to the condition of the wall, molding, and any other framework surrounding the window, such as the windowsill and window apron. Are there architectural details you'd like to enhance or imperfections you'd prefer to conceal? Based on what you see, determine if you prefer inside- or outside-mount curtains.

Inside-mount. Here, the hardware and curtains are contained within the inside dimensions of your window frame, with curtains no longer than the windowsill. Inside-mount curtains can help showcase beautiful woodwork around your window. This style also gives the curtains a more built-in, tailored look. Inside-mount is the perfect choice for a recessed window, a window type that is set back into the wall. It is also the perfect mounting for café curtains (see page 22) or curtains above furniture or radiators. Do keep in mind that when inside-mount curtains are drawn completely open, they will stack against the sides of the window, somewhat concealing the actual windowpanes and obstructing some natural light.

Outside-mount. In this approach, sometimes also called a face mount, the hardware and curtains are mounted directly to your wall or the molding above the window. Visually, outside-mount curtains give you the opportunity to play with scale and can even make windows appear larger, depending on curtain length and placement. Outside-mount curtains can be any length you choose, and they can pull open to one or both sides, depending on your preference. This type of mounting is the perfect solution to conceal unsightly window frames or other imperfections around your window. It's also great if you wish to disguise the overall shape of the window, or give the illusion of a larger window. Keep in mind that you will need to have at least 2" above the window (on either the wall or woodwork above the window) for mounting the hardware required to hang outside-mount curtains.

inside-mount curtains   outside-mount curtains

WINDOW COVERINGS DEFINED

You may hear the terms *drapery, curtains, window treatments, shades,* and *blinds,* among others, when referring to coverings for your windows. But what exactly are the nuances and differences, and can all these different terms be used interchangeably? The short answer: sometimes. The phrase *window treatment* refers to any kind of decoration used on, in, around, or over a window. Therefore, *window treatment* is the ubiquitous phrase used to define each and every type of window covering, from curtains, to blinds, to valances, and every variation in between. Let's further explore the many variations.

Draperies. These are used for more formal window coverings, are typically floor length, and are often operated using a relatively complex pulley-cord system to open and close them. Draperies completely frame a window when open and completely cover it when closed. Draperies are frequently a rather complicated construction using heading tape and hooks hung

drapery hooks

from a track or rod along the top edge. They are usually lined and are often characterized by an intricate pleating system whereby they are attached to the hardware. The pleats (or gathers) condense the width of the fabric *before* it is hung on the mounting hardware. Draperies are not covered in this book.

Curtains. These also hang from some sort of mounting hardware along the top edge, but they have a much more casual look and feel than draperies. They open and close by hand — a more simple operation. They are typically hung from rods using rings, clips, tabs, ties, or directly through a rod pocket casing. Unlike draperies, curtains are flat panels, and the width is condensed *after* it is hung. Curtains may also be lined, depending on your preference. You may choose to hang your curtains as single panels per window that draw open to one side, or in pairs, drawing open to both sides.

rod pocket casing

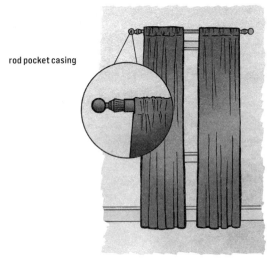

Sash curtains. These are very similar to curtains, the main distinction being that they are hung from a rod along both the top and bottom edges, keeping them drawn tightly closed and in place. They are primarily used for privacy in places such as windows set into doors or other windows where you would prefer your curtain be left closed, as you typically do not open sash curtains.

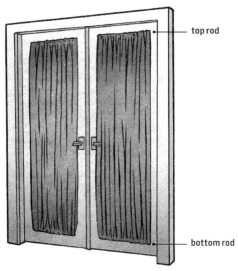

top rod

bottom rod

Shades. Often opaque, shades are used as a quick, easy way to cover a window. Shades can be hung using inside- or outside-mount techniques, although inside-mount is much more standard. Inside-mount shades are typically the actual width of the window frame and hang very smoothly when closed. Outside-mount shades rarely extend wider than the molding surrounding the window. A translucent shade filters and softens light.

Depending on the type, shades may roll up, gather up, or even pleat up (such as a Roman shade). Balloon shades billow, creating an opulent look with a series of shirred, curving arcs along the bottom edge. You may choose to open shades partially, revealing only some of the window and continuing to provide privacy and shade from the outside light. Often times, shades are operated on pull cords, so special consideration should be given to installing in homes with children. Note that it is also possible to purchase "cordless" shades to avoid strangulation risks and hazards.

Roman shade

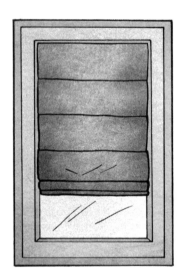

Blinds. Very similar to shades, blinds may be either translucent or opaque and are often made of metal, wood, or similar materials. The primary difference is that blinds typically function with a slat, venetian, or pleated honeycomb system, opening bottom to top, top to bottom, or side to side. If individual slats make up the blinds, the slats can typically be tilted to filter or block light to your preference. Blinds can be used alone or combined with another more decorative outside-mount curtain or drapery system. Like shades, they may operate on either a pull cord or cordless system.

blinds

Valances. When used alone, a valance is the perfect way to add a splash of color or pattern to your room without obstructing your window or blocking light and view. You may sometimes hear valances jokingly referred to as the miniskirt of the curtain world because they are short. Valances are also great to use over purchased basic shades and blinds to add a personal touch and help tie in the look with the room. This stationary panel is mounted above the window for decorative interest. A valance may also be used in conjunction with curtains or a drapery system. Valances are commonly 10" to 16" long. They are mounted much the same as curtains, with the same heading options (covered in chapter 2). When used in conjunction with a curtain, you may choose to use a double rod or a separate rod altogether, although the valance will typically conceal the rod or top of the shade of the main window covering.

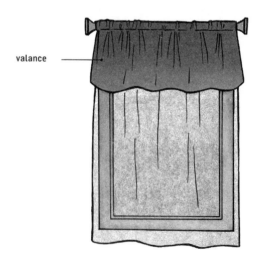

valance

Cornices. For lack of a better description, a cornice is a stationary, decorative, upholstered, backless, bottomless rectangular box, typically constructed of wood or foam and mounted at the top of a window to conceal the hardware used to hang curtains or draperies. The rigidity of a cornice differentiates it from a valance. The curtain or drapery used with a cornice is mounted to the wall, inside the cornice box, creating a more formal look. Like valances, cornices are also short, often 14" to 16" long. There is often a top on the cornice to help prevent dust from settling onto your curtains or drapery. The fabric used to cover the cornice is usually stapled in place over a layer of batting, which allows the fabric to be drawn tight and smoothed in place. You can purchase a cornice board kit, and this is often a no-sew project — simply staple and glue.

cornice

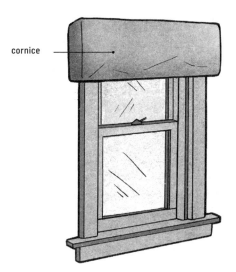

CHAPTER TWO

FROM THE TOP DOWN

When making and installing your curtains, you may find that the most significant details are along the top edge: the mounting hardware you use and how the curtain will hang from the rod. There are many options to consider when it comes to mounting hardware. Will you choose something simple and understated, sleek and modern, or more ornate? Once your hardware is in place, take the time to explore the various heading options. These are the styling details along the top hemmed edge of your window covering. There certainly is not a shortage of possibilities to make your custom curtains uniquely you!

FIXTURES AND HARDWARE

AT FIRST GLANCE, THE OPTIONS for curtain-mounting hardware can seem overwhelming, so let's break them down. For a start, curtains are traditionally hung from tracks, poles, or rods.

Tracks are functional, without much aesthetic appeal. They are generally used when working with drapery and are hidden behind the window treatment. Tracks will not be covered in this book.

Poles and **rods** can be decorative as well as functional. The terms tend to be used interchangeably without much differentiation, although technically speaking, curtain rods are adjustable in length, while curtain poles are fixed. For the sake of simplicity, this book will focus on the term *curtain rod*.

Where to Place the Curtain Rods?

There are few hard and fast rules about mounting hardware. Generally speaking, use your own judgment and install curtain rods where you find them most pleasing (for instance, on the wall above the window frame and molding, or directly on the molding). The placement you choose for your curtain rod can have quite a visual impact on the perception of window proportions. For example, mounting a curtain rod significantly higher and wider than the actual window can create the illusion of a much larger window.

Before installing your hardware, think about how you intend to use your curtains. For example, do you intend to leave them open, or might you open and close them frequently? When they are drawn open, would you prefer them hanging in front of the window slightly, or on the wall so they do not obstruct any natural sunlight? If the latter is the case, be sure to install your hardware so that when the curtains are drawn fully open, they sit on the wall (see Stackback Allowance on facing page).

If you are looking for some guidelines, here are a few to give you some ideas.

- Outside-mount rods are best placed anywhere from 2" to 8" above the window, extending approximately 4" to 6" or more on either side of the window molding.
- Most commonly, mounting brackets should be installed approximately 1" to 1¼" inside each end of the curtain rod, especially if you plan to hang your curtains from rings. This distance between the mounting brackets and the ends of the curtain rods allows just enough space for one curtain ring to fit and ensures that when the curtains are drawn fully open, they will pull right to the end of the rod.
- If there are multiple windows in one room, it is best to install all hardware the same distance above all the windows in the room to create visual unity and harmony.

Note that it is best to select your hardware prior to making curtains, as the finished length and width of the curtain will depend on the placement and dimensions of the specific hardware you choose.

Stackback Allowance

The length of the rod that extends beyond the width of the window is called the curtain *stackback* distance. This is the space along the sides of the window, on the wall, where the curtain rests when drawn fully open. One standard is to extend the rod approximately 15 percent of the width of the window beyond both sides of the window that you wish to expose. For example, if you are making curtains for a 36" wide window, the stackback distance on each side of the window would be approximately 5" (36" × 15% = 5.4").

Wider windows have wider curtains and will need a larger stackback to accommodate the curtain fabric when drawn fully open. Lightweight curtains require a smaller stackback distance because the fabric compresses more easily than heavyweight fabric when drawn open.

Types of Curtain Rods

When shopping, you may find the endless options for curtain rods overwhelming. The descriptions that follow should help take some of the guesswork out of making your final selection.

Curtain rods with or without finials. These come in a variety of lengths, diameters, widths, and materials, most commonly metal, wood, or plastic. They can be basic (smooth) or decorative (with a fluted texture), flat or round. Curtains rods may even have elbow pieces at each end so that the side edges of the curtain return to the wall, adding privacy, all the while preventing unwanted light or views.

Hardware Installation Tips

Pay careful attention when it comes time to install your preferred curtain-mounting system to the wall or window frame:

- Be sure to use a level to ensure that everything is perfectly horizontal and balanced.
- The material to which you attach your mounting hardware (wood, Sheetrock, plaster, masonry, and so on) will impact the type of screw or wall anchor you select. If you're not sure what to use, consult with your local hardware associate.
- Keep in mind not only the weight of the curtain but also the added weight applied when physically pulling the curtain open and closed. Be sure to use strong-enough anchors so that your curtain rod won't be pulled off the wall!

To further complicate the choices available to you, you may even find double and triple curtain rods, for hanging two layers of curtains or a curtain and a valance, for example. Rods are usually fixed to the wall above the window with brackets. If choosing a more decorative rod, you may wish to use complementary rings to attach the curtain so that you can also showcase your rod. Ultimately, you want to make sure that your finished curtains will move freely and smoothly along the length of the rod when in place.

basic rod

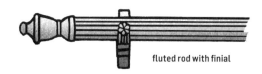

fluted rod with finial

elbow rod

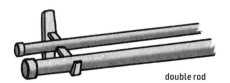

double rod

Café curtain rods. This type of rod is similar to a basic curtain rod. The main difference is that café curtain rods are adjustable and lightweight, making them the perfect choice for hanging café curtains and other lightweight curtains. Café rods are fixed flat to the window or wall, with either an inside- or outside-mount. These rods are typically not as thick as basic curtain rods and are mounted right at eye level. You should not hang heavy or long curtains on café rods, as the weight of the curtain may cause the rod to flex or bend.

inside-mount
café curtain rod

outside-mount
café curtain rod

Tension rods. This type of rod is adjustable with an internal spring to provide tension when the rod is placed between the side edges of a window frame; two rubber ends hold the tension rod in place. Typically used for an inside-mount, it's a perfect option when you don't want to see the fixture, as these are often very basic and intended to be concealed by the top edge of a rod pocket curtain.

spring tension rod with rubber ends

Tension wires. These have been around for a long time, but in recent years, tension wires have become sleeker and more commonly used. They are constructed of a fine-coiled metal wire, which is often coated. The wire may be threaded through the curtain casing or eyelets, or the curtain may be hung in place through the use of clips or other curtain-hanging options. Depending on the application, tension wires often provide a more modern look.

tension wires

Additional Hardware

Once you have determined your preferred curtain-mounting system, ask yourself the following questions to decide if additional hardware is needed with your curtain rod.

- Does the curtain rod come with mounting hardware or do I need to purchase brackets separately?
- Does the rod require decorative end caps that must be purchased separately?
- Will I need rings or clips to hang my curtains from the rod?
- Will I need additional hardware to hold the curtains open (such as tiebacks or holdbacks)?

Read on to consider these options, then, later in this chapter, review the various curtain heading styles, which explain how to actually hang the curtain from the rod.

Brackets. As noted above, not all curtain rods come with mounting hardware. If selecting a decorative rod, you may need to purchase mounting brackets separately. Brackets can be anything from basic to ornamental. Whatever you choose, make sure that the bracket you select is appropriate for and can accommodate your curtain rod. It is best to buy these items at the same time to ensure a good fit.

bracket variations

Finials. Some curtain rods come with fixed end pieces, while others require the additional purchase of decorative end pieces, called finials. These caps finish the ends of the curtain rod and prevent the curtains from sliding off. Finials range from ornate acorns, leaves, and fleur-de-lis designs to simple round balls. You may find it easiest to purchase finials from the same line as the curtain rod you choose, which guarantees a matching finish and good fit.

finial variations

Rings. If you are not planning to hang your curtain using one of the heading styles described later in this chapter, or if you are using a more decorative curtain rod that you wish to showcase, rings are the most common method of hanging the curtain on the rod. Rings come in a variety of materials and often coordinate with the curtain rod. Most important is to make sure that the rings you choose can accommodate the circumference of the curtain rod, ensuring ease of movement when opening and closing the curtain. Curtain rings often have eyelets on the bottom edge and are sewn directly to the top edge of the curtains.

Clips. These are simple and easy to use, allowing you to quickly hang your curtains. Clips glide easily along the rod or tension wire and come in a wide variety of styles. Like rings, you want to make sure that the clips you choose can accommodate the curtain rod. They are the perfect option for curtains that may need to be laundered regularly. Clips are also a great option for no-sew curtains (see page 113), when you choose to use something ready-made, such as a sheet or tablecloth, for your curtains.

Holdbacks. As with curtain rods, holdbacks vary greatly in style and material. The primary function is to do just what the name suggests: hold back an open curtain. The holdback may be anything from a basic knob to a decorative arm. Regardless of styling, the holdback will be mounted to the wall. You may choose to mount (and even select) your preferred holdback after your finished curtains are in place so you can evaluate whether you will be satisfied with placement and styling. Work with a friend to determine the best placement height for the holdback, as the final location will impact the silhouette of the curtains when they are open. When the curtains are fully closed, the holdback should be completely concealed.

holdback variations

Tiebacks. Although not technically "hardware," a tieback is an alternative to a holdback and is used to tie the curtains back from the window when open. Again, placement is based on personal preference, although as a general rule, it is usually best not to place them dead center at the side of the window. Move them higher and lower to see what you prefer. Tiebacks placed higher along the edge of a window will allow more light to enter the room because it will hold more of the curtain out of the way.

Tiebacks can be simple or opulent (with fringe, tassels, and more), depending on your preference. You will often need to purchase additional hardware to secure your tieback to the wall. This can be a simple hook or a tieback holder that coordinates with your curtain rod. If choosing to make a tieback, your fabric needs can be calculated when selecting and purchasing your curtain fabric. If making your own, tiebacks are typically interfaced to add stability and keep them looking crisp. (For how-to instructions, see Fabric Tiebacks on page 115.)

HEADING STYLES

ONCE YOU HAVE DETERMINED your preferred curtain rod style and mounting system, consider the different curtain heading options. A *heading* refers to the hemmed top edge of a window covering — the means by which the curtain is attached to the rod. The most straightforward approach is to hang your curtain directly on the rod using a basic rod pocket casing, tabs, or ties. Otherwise, you may choose to attach the curtain to the rod with rings or clips. In short, there are a variety of different heading styles you may want to consider. Choose a heading style before calculating (and cutting) your fabric yardage to ensure that you will have enough fabric for the style you choose.

Rod pocket casing. This heading style has a channel stitched along the top edge of a curtain, through which you directly insert the curtain rod. Traditional rod pocket casing curtains are not intended to be open and closed frequently, but rather to be left open through the use of tiebacks or holdbacks. With this in mind, they typically fit snugly on the rod and, as a result,

wrong side

basic rod pocket casing

have a great deal of friction when opening. Alternatively, you may also make a more relaxed rod pocket casing, which would be quite a bit larger than the curtain rod, making the casing more functional and conducive to opening and closing.

A casing may also have a header that extends above the rod, creating a ruffle along the top edge of the curtain above the casing. Ruffled headers are anywhere from 1" to 5" tall, depending on the desired look and structure of the fabric. For example, a more structured fabric can support a taller header, while a drapier fabric requires a shorter header so it does not droop. Headers are optional decorative details.

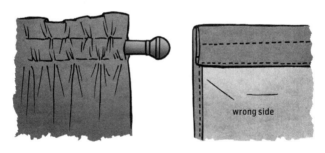

rod pocket casing with ruffled header

You may also choose to add a separate fabric to the top edge of the curtain to create the casing. This is a way to introduce a contrast fabric or color, or a way to play with pattern (if your curtains are vertical stripes, perhaps you would like the stripes on the rod pocket to run horizontally). It's a great way to have some fun, without being too over-the-top.

Tab top. This heading style features individual fabric loops along the curtain's upper edge instead of a casing. A more decorative rod is commonly used with this heading style, as the rod will be visible in between the individual tabs. Tabs are sometimes secured with buttons for a decorative look, but if you are planning to use buttons, opt to keep the curtains short (such as a café length) in order to prevent the buttonholes from pulling out of shape from the weight of the curtains. If you wish to use buttons on longer-length curtains, simply stitch the buttons in place to the base of the tabs without the use of buttonholes. This makes the buttons decorative instead of functional, adding to the longevity of your curtains. Tabs are a great choice for curtains that you intend to open and close frequently.

tab top

Hidden tab. This heading style is kind of a cross between the rod pocket casing and the tab top. When closed, hidden tab top curtains create subtle, soft, even pleats. When open, this heading style allows the curtain to stack nicely on itself, creating a slightly more formal look, similar to a drapery. The top edge of the curtain is hemmed much like a rod pocket casing, but tabs are then added to the back side of the casing at designated intervals. The tabs are not visible from the right side of the curtain, creating a very clean look. The curtain rod itself is inserted directly through each hidden tab.

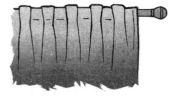

hidden tab, front view

hidden tab, back view

Tie top. Similar to tab top curtains, these are also individual fabric strips sewn in place along the top edge of the curtain. Tie top curtains have a somewhat more relaxed feel, as the individual ties are casually knotted or tied into bows to hang the curtain. The ties may be attached directly to the rod or to curtain rings. Using fabric or even ribbon (such as grosgrain), the ties can be made any length. Before making the actual ties, it's a good idea to use scraps of fabric to test your preferred length and make sure they will tie to your liking. The width of the ties is also a factor from both a visual perspective (how they will look on the curtain rod) as well as a functional point of view (to ensure they fit, if attaching to curtain rings).

tie top

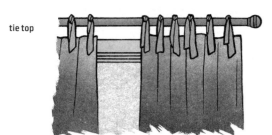

Scalloped edge. When you are looking for something a touch out of the ordinary, a scalloped edge along the top of a curtain provides a simple decoration. The scallops are created with a deep hem along the top edge of the curtain and a simple circle template. This type of heading is best suited for stationary panels and a curtain width that is typically the actual width of the window, as this will help showcase the scallops. The peaks in between each scallop are hung on the curtain rod in a variety of ways, including rings, tabs, or ties.

scalloped edge

Grommets or eyelets. This sleek heading style features soft pleats when both open and closed. To execute this heading, use a tool to set the grommets (or eyelets) in place along the top edge of the curtain panel; the rod is then inserted directly through each opening. The difference between the two is that eyelets are one piece (set on the front only) and are used for lighter-weight fabrics; grommets are two pieces that work together (one set on the front of the fabric, the other on the back) and are used for heavier-weight fabrics. You can find both metal and plastic options in different sizes and finishes. Plastic grommets are often much larger, easier to install, and come in a wide variety of decorative color choices. These are a great choice for shower curtains.

rod inserted through grommets

Buttonholes. This heading style functions much like a grommet, but instead of using additional hardware, vertical buttonholes are stitched along the top edge of the hemmed curtain panel at specific intervals, based on the curtain's width. The curtain rod is then threaded through each individual buttonhole to hang the curtain in place. This is a good choice if you like the look and drape of a grommet heading but don't want to add any hardware.

Heading tapes. These are ready-made tapes that are stitched directly to the wrong side of the folded, finished top edge of the curtain. These tapes are very useful when you wish to simplify the pleating (or ruffling) process. Nearly all heading tapes feature strings to pull, which result in even gathers, pleats, or ruffles. Using this tape helps take some of the math out of the pleating equation. You will also need the appropriate plastic or metal hooks to hang the curtain to your mounting fixture. It is best to purchase all of these items together, so you are sure to get what you need to complete your project. The type of heading tape you select will affect the amount of fabric you need. You can typically follow the manufacturer's instructions included with the heading tape to determine the correct fabric width to purchase.

Pleated. Pleats are traditionally used in draperies to gather the top edge of the fabric before it is hung. When it comes to pleating styles, there is definitely not a shortage. You can find pinch pleats, goblet pleats, French pleats, smocked pleats, and inverted pleats, to name just a handful. The majority are individually calculated and made by hand without the use of special heading tapes. Pleat styles fall into one of two camps: *extroverted* (those that stand away from the drapery fabric) and *introverted* (pleats that lie flat against it). A pleated heading is probably the most complicated to execute due to the sheer variety, as well as the extensive math and hand-stitching it requires.

CHAPTER THREE

FABRICS, LENGTHS, AND LININGS

Every room in your home has great makeover potential. With new custom curtains, you can make the transformation happen while you beautifully frame your view. Adding or changing window treatments instantly changes any room. Curtains allow you to play with color, pattern, and scale, as well as reflect your personal style and design sensibility. Use your new window treatments to pull together the elements in the room and create ambience. You can control light, add privacy, obscure a boring view, stop or limit drafts, and sometimes even dampen sound.

CHOOSING YOUR FABRIC

THE FIRST ESSENTIAL STEP in making your curtains is to choose the fabric that is right for you. There are so many beautiful options in a dazzling range of color, pattern, and texture. Think about your application: Are you looking to make sheers to help diffuse the light? Or do you want a less transparent fabric for a greater degree of privacy? Are you mainly looking for an opportunity to infuse some color and pattern into your home?

Generally speaking, you are going to want to choose a woven fabric without stretch. That means staying away from knits, which tend to droop and sag. For all applications, your best fabric choices are going to be woven cottons, linens, silks, or voiles, and they could be anything from lightweight to home dec weight.

Consider whether you intend to machine-wash or dry-clean your finished curtains, as this may impact your fabric choice. If machine washing is your desired method, cotton is recommended, but be sure to prewash your fabric before making your curtains to avoid shrinkage later. Cotton is also a great choice because it has fabulous longevity, unlike some silks, which will have a tendency to rot with time, especially when exposed to extreme sunlight. Also note that some fabrics, such as linen, might turn yellow over time from sun exposure, though this can often be reversed with patience and special cleaning.

Other than basic laundering and dry cleaning, a couple other tried-and-true methods of caring for your finished curtains are simply airing them out on a clothesline on a breezy day or vacuuming them with the appropriate vacuum-cleaner attachment.

Once you have decided on a type of fabric, look at a large piece of it under natural light. If possible, hang your fabric choices in front of the store window and see how they will naturally drape and fold. Try to view the fabric from the same distance that you would see it in your home. Sometimes patterned fabrics take on quite a different look from different perspectives. Colors can also change quite a bit when the fabric is illuminated from the back by natural sunlight. This would also be the time to decide whether or not to add a lining or interlining fabric (see page 42) to your curtains. If so, layer your fabrics and view them in the store window to help finalize your decision.

Better still would be to look at the fabric you intend to use for your curtains in the actual room you plan to hang it. Although this is not always possible, it is an ideal way to accurately gauge color, scale, and overall aesthetic appeal. Depending on the fabric you'd like to use, it may be a worthwhile investment to purchase a yard to take home with you. You can always use this extra fabric to make tiebacks (see page 115) or even accent pillows.

CLASSIC CURTAIN LENGTHS

THERE ARE ENDLESS OPTIONS when it comes to curtain lengths. Ultimately, the length you choose will give you the opportunity to play with proportion. For example, floor-length curtains can make a small window appear much taller. Similarly, using a wide outside-mount installation for a small window will make the window appear wider. Placing a deep valance or cornice somewhat higher than the window can make it look taller.

There are standard rules that you may choose to follow when creating classic length curtains, or you may choose to break from the standards. Feel free to follow your own creative instincts and make your custom curtains the length that looks right to you. Keep in mind that, generally speaking, longer lengths tend to create a more formal look. Also, consider the frequency of opening and closing, location, and the overall styling of your space.

Sill length. As the name implies, a sill-length curtain hangs just to the top of the windowsill. It is the perfect length for windows located above furniture or radiators, or windows that are regularly opened. You may also find this length most suitable for small rooms, high-traffic areas, and kitchens. Sill-length curtains are the least intrusive, and the easiest to operate, making this the perfect length for curtains that you plan to open and close frequently.

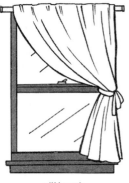

sill length

Café curtains. This variation on sill length is typically half of the window height and covers the lower half of the window. Café curtains provide some privacy without compromising natural light. They are the perfect choice for casual settings, such as kitchen windows. You may choose to hang two sets of café curtains for a tiered look, with one set covering the lower window and the other set covering the upper window. Tiered café curtains are quite versatile in that you can choose which portion to open and close.

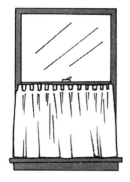

café curtains

Apron length. This length falls typically at least 4" below the windowsill. As the name implies, this length of curtain covers the window apron. As with sill length curtains, you may find that apron length is also a good choice above furniture, radiators, and so forth. If you want to conceal unattractive woodwork without the weight of a floor-length curtain, this might be your best bet.

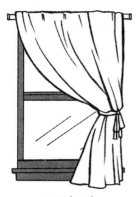

apron length

Floor length. The standard for this length is ½" above the surface of the floor, which creates a more formal look. Measure carefully, as anything shorter than ½" may look awkwardly too short. Floor-length curtains are ideal for more formal settings, bay windows, and sliding glass doors. They are also the perfect choice if you have smaller windows but want to create a more grand effect.

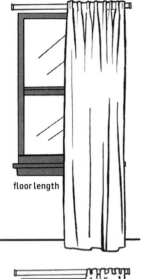

floor length

Slight break. The finished length of this more sophisticated curtain is 1" to 6" longer than floor length, resulting in a small puddle on the floor. This curtain length requires quite a bit of maintenance and should be given the same considerations as puddle length, below.

Puddle. Just as the name implies, puddle-length curtains allow an extra 6" to 10" of curtain fabric to pool on the floor. This is the perfect choice for floor-to-ceiling windows when you are looking to produce a dramatic effect. This curtain length is *not* recommended for high-traffic areas, windows that are frequently

slight break

opened, or homes with pets or small children. Generally speaking, they require quite a bit of maintenance to make sure that they puddle in place "just so."

Valance. A valance is more of a top treatment as opposed to an actual curtain, but it's definitely worth mentioning, as you may opt for this type of window styling, used alone or in conjunction with a longer curtain. A valance is hung at the top of a window and is typically between 10" and 16" long; as a general rule, it should not be more than one-third of the length of the actual window. Used alone, a valance offers a splash of color and pattern without sacrificing the view or natural light. You may use it in conjunction with another curtain for visual interest, and in a different (complementary or contrasting) pattern. Valances are also great choices to help liven up the appearance of basic shades and blinds. Functionally, a valance can help conceal rods and hardware or even an irregular curtain heading.

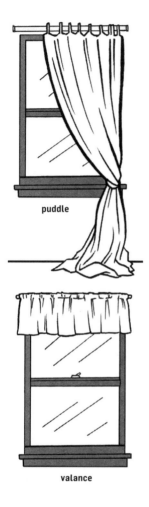

puddle

valance

TYPES OF LINING

WHILE DRAPERIES ARE ALWAYS LINED, curtains are only sometimes lined. That said, there are definite benefits to lining your curtains, depending on the look and function you are trying to achieve. Although adding linings takes more time and effort when you are making your curtains, linings do add to the longevity of your window coverings.

Unlined curtains. These function primarily as decor and provide limited privacy. Unlined curtains diffuse daylight and provide some privacy from the outside world during the day. Depending on the fabric weight, however, people outside might be able to see in at night when the lights are on inside the room. Unlined curtains are certainly quick, easy, and economical to make. They are also more casual than lined curtains. Although there are benefits, the life span of unlined curtains is shorter than that of lined, as they may be damaged by sun exposure more quickly. Sometimes, direct sun exposure may even cause fabric to develop a yellowish tint over time.

Lined curtains. There are many benefits to lined curtains. On an aesthetic level, linings add weight and body to the curtains, helping them hang better and stay put, improving shape, and enhancing their overall look. Linings also add additional stability to the heading and hemmed side edges. Functionally, linings add opaqueness, provide some insulation, and help protect furniture and other items in your room from the sun. Lining will also give your curtains a longer life by protecting the main fabric from fading and deterioration.

Depending on the lining you choose, a lined curtain can also provide a somewhat more formal look to your finished curtains. Ideally, the lining will last as long as the curtain itself, but depending on the lining you choose and the conditions of the space (for example, exposure to direct sunlight or condensation and humidity from an open window or in a bathroom), you may notice that with time, the lining eventually begins to wear out, but this will happen before your main curtain fabric does. If this occurs, you may choose to remove the lining altogether and either leave the curtains unlined or reline them to further extend their life.

Interlined curtains. Just as the name implies, an *interlining* is sewn between the exterior and lining layers of your curtains. The primary function of interlining is to increase the life span of your curtains. Interlining will also provide added insulation, sound-dampening properties, and additional light-blocking attributes. Not surprisingly, though, interlined curtains are more complicated to make than basic lined curtains. You might find it easier to invest in linings that already have the attributes that fit your specific needs. Interlining fabrics are almost always cotton, and most commonly flannel or some other brushed material, because the brushed surface will help hold heat and dampen sound.

Best Fabrics for Linings

When choosing a lining fabric, you may want something that is specifically designated as a lining fabric. Such fabrics are often cheaper than your main curtain fabric and are loaded with helpful attributes, such as being stain repellent, water resistant, crease resistant, and more. Lining fabrics are typically a plain- or sateen-weave construction (a sateen-weave fabric flows and drapes somewhat more freely than plain weave), 100 percent cotton or a polyester/cotton blend, and have a crisper feel than your average fabric, ensuring that they hang well.

Traditionally, you'll want to go with a white or off-white fabric so that it does not affect the look of your main curtain fabric when light shines through it. White linings will also create a visual uniformity when looking at your windows from the outside. If you do wish to select a colored or contrast fabric for a lining, it would be best to get samples of both your curtain and lining fabric and hold them together up to a light source to make sure that the color of your main curtain fabric does not change, or that you are pleased with the effect if it does. Generally speaking, a mid- to heavy-weight lining fabric will hang better and provide a fuller, less wrinkled, finished look to your curtains.

There are literally hundreds of different linings available to purchase on the market. Think about the needs of your space and your home as you explore the many options. For example, you may want a blackout lining for the curtains in your child's room, especially if he or she is a very early riser or has difficulty falling asleep at night. The simple addition of this lining could make a difference. A handful of readily available functional lining fabrics include the following:

- blackout lining
- thermal or insulating lining
- reflective lining
- sound-dampening lining
- climate-control lining

When making your final decision about lining fabric, consider the curtain fabric you have selected. Ideally, the lining will have a similar construction so they hang well together. The two fabrics you select may have different cleaning requirements, so pay close attention to this when it comes time to have your curtains laundered. For example, if the curtain fabric is machine washable, but the lining is dry-clean only, the finished curtains should only be dry-cleaned (as needed) to keep the fabrics looking compatible. Before making your curtains, always take the time up front to select the best lining to fit your needs.

CHAPTER FOUR

MEASURING UP

Curtains do not need to be complicated. The beauty of making your own curtains is that it depends less on sewing skills (after all, you're pretty much hemming rectangles) and more on taking precise measurements and making thoughtful use of fabric and style. As an added bonus, because you will be designing custom window treatments, they can be crafted to fit your specific windows. The fabric, the lining, the length, the drape, and all the little details that make it fabulous are in your complete control. You can take pride and pleasure in knowing that you won't find a window treatment exactly like it anywhere else. Discover the rewards of designing and creating your own unique look for your bathroom, living room, bedroom, kitchen, and every other room in between!

TAKING ACCURATE WINDOW MEASUREMENTS

BEFORE TAKING YOUR ACTUAL window measurements, finalize your curtain rod hardware, mounting preference, and location (see chapter 2 for hardware hanging specifics). Then go ahead and do the actual hardware installation. You want your fixtures in place because it will always be easier and more accurate to take your curtain measurements from an installed curtain rod. Start measurements from the top edge of the rod, unless you intend to hang your curtains from rings or clips.

Once your hanging hardware is mounted to your wall or window, depending on your personal preference, and you have decided on your finished curtain length, let's get down to the business of measuring for your custom curtains. For absolute accuracy, use a metal tape measure. If you are a frequent sewer, you may automatically grab your flexible quilter's tape measure for the task — don't do it. A fabric tape measure will flex and bend, and your measurements are more likely to be inaccurate, resulting in wonky window coverings.

Here are four other important tips to follow to ensure accurate measurements:

1. Round all numbers to the nearest $\frac{1}{8}$". This level of accuracy is particularly necessary when measuring for inside-mount curtains to successfully create a "built-in," tailored look.

2. Measure every window for which you plan to make curtains, especially for inside-mount curtains. Even if two

windows are side by side in the same room and appear to be visually identical, you may find that the measurements vary in width or length or even both, especially in older homes.

3. Always take measurements in more than one location. For example, when measuring the width for an inside-mount curtain, measure the inside width in three places: the top third, middle, and bottom third of the window opening. Doing so will help guarantee an accurate fit for your curtains. If you do find a variation between the three measurements, use the narrowest measurement for your final number. When measuring for length, measure the window vertically in the center of the window, left of center, and right of center. In nearly all cases, note the shortest dimension to determine your finished length for both outside-mount and inside-mount curtains. If possible, you may want to enlist a helper to assist you in the task of measuring.

4. Measure everything twice! The extra time you spend double-checking your measurements up front will certainly pay off in your finished window coverings!

Refer to the diagrams and charts for inside- and outside-mount curtains to accurately measure your window dimensions (see pages 49–51). These measurements will help you determine the finished dimensions of your curtains.

Measuring for Inside-Mount Curtains

Inside width of window in three places (circle the narrowest measurement)

WIDTH 1:

WIDTH 2:

WIDTH 3:

Inside length in three places, from top edge of curtain rod to windowsill (circle the shortest measurement)

LENGTH 1:

LENGTH 2:

LENGTH 3:

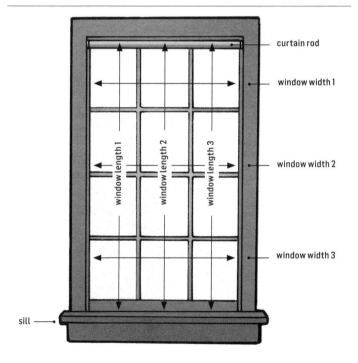

curtain rod

window width 1

window length 1

window length 2

window length 3

window width 2

window width 3

sill

Measuring for Outside-Mount Curtains

Width of curtain rod, from bracket to bracket

MEASUREMENT: _____

Sill length: length from top edge of curtain rod (or from bottom of rings or clips, if using) to the sill

MEASUREMENT 1: _____

MEASUREMENT 2: _____

MEASUREMENT 3: _____

(Circle the shortest measurement.)

Apron length: length from top edge of curtain rod (or from bottom of rings or clips, if using) to bottom edge of the apron (or desired length below apron)

MEASUREMENT 1: _____

MEASUREMENT 2: _____

MEASUREMENT 3: _____

(Circle the longest measurement.)

Floor length: length from top edge of curtain rod (or from bottom of rings or clips, if using) to the floor (less ½")

MEASUREMENT 1: _____

MEASUREMENT 2: _____

MEASUREMENT 3: _____

(Circle the shortest measurement.)

Custom length: measure the height of curtain you'd like for your finished length. This should be from the top edge of the curtain rod (or from bottom of rings or clips, if using) down to your desired finished edge

MEASUREMENT: _____

MEASURING FOR OUTSIDE-MOUNT CURTAINS*

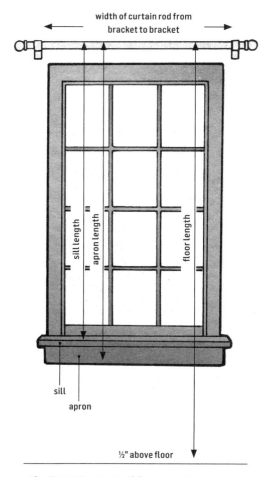

width of curtain rod from
bracket to bracket

sill length

apron length

floor length

sill

apron

½" above floor

*See illustration on page 49 for an example on how to
accurately space the three length measurements.

STRUCTURAL ELEMENTS OF CURTAINS

NOW THAT YOU HAVE TAKEN the appropriate window measurements, it's also important to familiarize yourself with the basic structural elements of a curtain. Here are a handful of terms to know.

Heading allowance. This is only determined for rod pocket curtains and is the extra amount of fabric that you will need to go around the rod, allowing the curtain to move freely and smoothly over it. It is determined by measuring the circumference of the curtain rod and adding at least ½" to this measurement for ease. For a more relaxed look and functional casing (an absolute must if you intend to open and close the curtain frequently), you will want to make the casing height at least 1" larger than the circumference of the curtain rod, if not more.

Return. This is the portion of the curtain that extends from the end of the rod and folds back to the wall to block unwanted sunlight and view. A return is automatically created when using an elbow curtain rod — it's the portion of the rod that bends back to the wall. Otherwise, a return is not standard when using straight curtain rods; it is a matter of personal preference and is only possible for outside-mount curtains. For straight curtain rods, the return is calculated by measuring the distance from the center of the rod to the wall (in other words, measure the length of the mounting bracket from the wall to the center of the rod). For more on adding a return allowance, see Creating a Return Allowance for Straight Rods on page 90.

RETURN ALLOWANCE

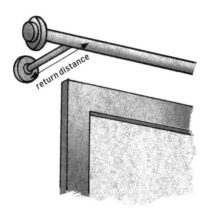

return distance

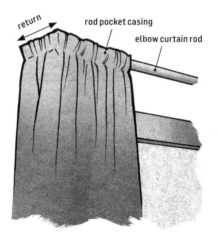

return

rod pocket casing

elbow curtain rod

Stackback allowance. Sometimes also called the left and right extension, this allowance is the area on the wall occupied by the curtain when it is drawn completely open. The length the curtain rod extends beyond the edges of the window defines this distance. Only outside-mount curtains have a stackback allowance. An appropriate stackback allowance guarantees that when the curtains are drawn completely open, they will not obstruct the window. (See Stackback Allowance on page 19.)

Curtain drop. This is the finished length from the top hemmed edge to the bottom hemmed edge of the curtain.

Leading edge. These are the inside vertical edges of the curtain, where they meet in the center of a window. This is typically the edge of the curtain that is pulled to draw the curtains open.

CURTAIN ANATOMY

return (see page 53)

heading allowance

stackback
allowance

leading
edge

curtain drop

CHAPTER FIVE

CALCULATING YARDAGE

In the simplest of terms, your fabric yardage for each curtain will be based on two basic measurements: finished curtain width and finished curtain length. In addition to the window measurements you took in the previous chapter, there are four additional factors that impact fabric yardage requirements: curtain fullness (refer to the chart on the facing page), heading style (which you have hopefully decided on), finished curtain length (also known as *curtain drop*), and matching pattern repeats (if necessary, depending on the fabric you have chosen).

CURTAIN FULLNESS

YOU'VE PROBABLY NOTICED that some curtains appear more gathered than others. Sometimes curtains hung on narrower windows are less full than those hung on wider windows and tend to be associated with less formal settings. You may also want to consider the print on the fabric when choosing fullness, as large prints tend to work better with less fullness.

Fullness measurements are not set in stone and can vary from curtain to curtain to achieve different effects. If you are at a loss for what will look best, you needn't worry; there are standards in place to help you. Curtain fullness is determined in direct relation to the width of the curtain rod. Follow the chart (below) or simply use it as a guideline to determine your ideal fullness when making your own custom curtains.

Curtain Fullness Guidelines

Although the standards below are tried and true, generally the lighter your fabric choice, the fuller you may go. For example, a curtain made of lace or voile can be cut and gathered to three times the window width. On the other hand, a heavier home dec–weight fabric might work better cut and gathered to a maximum of twice the window width. Try draping your fabric over a curtain rod and gathering it by hand to see what appeals most to you.

Tailored	1 × curtain rod width
Standard (traditional)	2 × curtain rod width
Full	2.5 × curtain rod width

CURTAIN WIDTH

Now that you have decided on curtain fullness, you can calculate the total fabric width required for your custom curtains. The only additional measurements you will need to take into account are the return allowances, if desired for your curtains (see page 52), and the side hem allowances. Simply follow the steps below to finalize the amount of fabric required to execute your desired curtain width. (See chart on page 66.)

1. Measure across the width of your mounted curtain rod from bracket to bracket (A).

2. Add twice the side return allowance distance (B) to this measurement, if using. (Remember, a return allowance is optional, unless you are using an elbow rod. See pages 52–53.)

3. Multiply this number by your desired fullness (tailored, standard, full, or other) (C).

4. If making two curtain panels, divide this number in half to determine the finished width of each curtain panel.

5. Add a standard 2" side hem allowance to your final number (to allow for a ½" double-fold side hem along both side edges, see page 73). Voilà! You now know your curtain panel width!

Here's an example for making full curtains with a return allowance:

1. Curtain rod width (A), measured bracket to bracket, is 38".

2. Return allowance (B) is 3", therefore, 38" + (2 × 3") = 44".

3. Desired fullness (C) is 2.5 (refer to the fullness chart on page 57), therefore, 44" × 2.5 = 110".

4. There will be two curtain panels, therefore, 110" ÷ 2 = 55".

5. Add the side hem allowance, therefore, 55" + 2" = 57" width per curtain panel.

Here's another example for making full curtains, omitting the return allowance (B):

1. Curtain rod width (A), measured bracket to bracket, is 38".

2. Desired fullness (C) is 2.5 (refer to the fullness chart on page 57), therefore, 38" × 2.5 = 95".

3. There will be two curtain panels, therefore 95" ÷ 2 = 47½".

4. Add the side hem allowance, therefore, 47½" + 2" = 49½" width per curtain panel (for simplicity, feel free to round up or down to the nearest whole number — either 49" or 50").

If your curtain panel width exceeds the width of your chosen fabric, you'll need to determine how many fabric widths are required to complete each curtain. There are two ways to do this:

1. One is to divide the calculated curtain panel width by the width of the fabric. For example, if the fabric width is 42", but your curtain panel width is 57", the calculation is 57" ÷ 42" = 1.36, meaning you will need nearly 1.5 widths of fabric for each panel.

2. Another way is to subtract the fabric width from the calculated panel width and see how much is left over. Using the same example, subtract 42" from 57", which indicates you need one fabric width plus another 15".

Working Chart to Record Your Width Measurements

If your required number of fabric widths ends up being just over or under a full width of fabric, it is easiest to adjust that number accordingly to simplify the process. For example, assume your calculations yield a 44" curtain panel width, but your fabric is only 42" wide. Simply revise your curtain panel width to 42" to save yourself the trouble of piecing panels together — not to mention the money you will save from not having to buy extra yardage! You'll never notice if your finished curtain is a few inches wider or narrower than the fullness you previously calculated, unless you are creating a tailored curtain (the exact width of the window), in which case you should go with the exact width you calculate.

(A) Curtain rod width (bracket to bracket)   _____

(B) Return allowance (optional)   _____

(C) Desired fullness   _____

Finished curtain panel width   _____

Side hem allowance (2" is standard)   _____

Required width of fabric, per curtain panel   _____

CURTAIN LENGTH

NOW THAT YOU HAVE DETERMINED curtain width, let's move on to determining the necessary length of the fabric required. This has a few more variables and considerations than width.

To determine total yardage per curtain panel, you first add the heading and hem allowances to the curtain length. If you have not yet finalized your heading and hem details but are dead set on purchasing your fabric, it's generally safe to add between 8" and 12" to the total length. This should allow you enough fabric to play with (plus a little extra) and ensure you achieve the look you are going for. If you do, in fact, have the heading and hem styling details finalized, read on to determine your total fabric length. As previously mentioned, measure twice and cut once to prevent fabric waste!

Heading allowance. Your choice of heading style (see chapter 2) for the curtains will impact your fabric yardage requirements. To determine the fabric allowance required for a plain rod pocket casing, measure the circumference of the rod, add ½" for turning back the raw edge, and another ½" minimum for ease to pull it over the rod. This will provide a snug-fitting casing, ideal for curtains that will stay either open or closed. For curtains that you intend to open and close frequently, you may desire a more relaxed and open rod pocket. If this is the case, determine what is visually pleasing to you, and add this additional heading allowance (at least 1") to your total curtain length. Decorative headers are typically only added to a more snugly fitting casing, to help ensure that the header stands properly. If you are also choosing to add a header (the optional extension of fabric that forms a ruffle above the casing), add twice the desired header height to your heading allowance measurement.

Hem allowance. Standard hem depth is typically 2". For medium- to heavyweight fabrics (such as quilting weight or home dec–weight fabrics), add 2½" to your curtain length to allow for the hem. For lighter-weight fabrics, such as linens or voiles, add 4" to your curtain length for hem allowance, so that you can make a deeper double-fold hem (see page 73). This will keep the cut edge of the fabric from showing through lighter-weight fabrics. This deep double-fold hem will also add a little more body and weight along the bottom edge of your curtains. Do keep in mind that a 2" hem is merely a guideline; you may certainly choose a wider or narrower hem based on the visual aesthetic you wish to achieve.

The required yardage length per curtain panel would be the finished length + the heading allowance + the hem allowance. As previously noted, if you haven't decided 100 percent on your preferred heading style and hem height, it's generally safe to add between 8" and 12" to the total length.

If you are using a solid fabric, you're all set to cut your fabric. If you are using a patterned fabric, read on about matching pattern repeats on page 65 before purchasing anything, as it will impact how much fabric will be required per curtain panel.

Working Chart to Record Your Length Measurements

Finished length (curtain drop)　　　　　　　　_____

+ Heading allowance　　　　　　　　_____

+ Hem allowance　　　　　　　　_____

= Total yardage (cut length) per curtain panel　　_____

UNSEWN CURTAIN PANEL

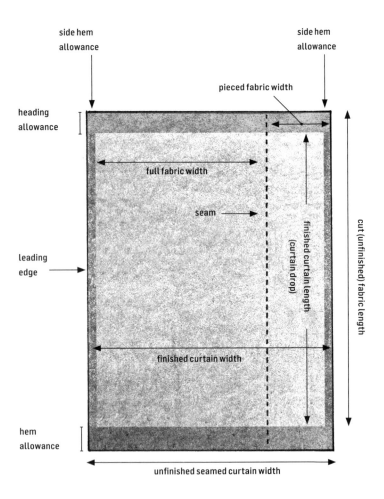

side hem allowance

side hem allowance

pieced fabric width

heading allowance

full fabric width

seam

finished curtain length (curtain drop)

cut (unfinished) fabric length

leading edge

finished curtain width

hem allowance

unfinished seamed curtain width

MATCHING PATTERN REPEATS

ALL PATTERNED FABRIC FEATURES one or more motifs that repeat at the same intervals all over the fabric. The rate at which the motifs duplicate (a combination of repeating both horizontally and vertically) is called a *repeat*. To further complicate things, all repeat sizes will differ from fabric to fabric. Matching repeats from curtain panel to curtain panel is not incredibly complicated, but does take some understanding, planning, and math to ensure you purchase the right amount of fabric. It may be unimportant to take into consideration the pattern repeats for small motifs, but it's worthwhile to think it through, as follows.

If space permits, open up a large piece of fabric, drape it in place in front of a window, so as to simulate your desired curtain fullness, and step back. How obvious is the pattern repeat? Your answer will help you determine if you should take the time to figure the pattern repeat into the equation when designing and making your curtains. If, while looking at the fabric, you're on the fence about whether or not to calculate yardage based on the repeat, then chances are you should take the repeat into consideration. This will help ensure that you will be happy with your curtains once they are finished and hanging in place.

If the fabric you choose has a bold, dramatic pattern, there's no question about what to do. Take the time to make your curtain panels match left to right and top to bottom, so that the same motifs fall along the same horizontal line. If you are making curtains for more than one window in the same room out of the same fabric, each curtain panel should match, with the repeat being positioned at the same location in each panel. You will thank yourself later for the time you spent making this happen; your finished results will be much more visually pleasing and look professional.

To determine the repeat of the fabric you have chosen, use a ruler to measure the actual vertical repeat on your desired fabric. Note a specific motif in the pattern design and insert a straight pin at this location to mark it. Measure the vertical distance until this same motif repeats itself again, and you will have determined your vertical repeat distance. Follow the same technique to find the horizontal repeat.

FINDING AND MEASURING THE PATTERN REPEAT

It can be somewhat daunting to determine your yardage per curtain panel when taking fabric repeats into consideration. Follow these five steps and you'll have your yardage requirements in no time, and your curtain panels will match perfectly from top to bottom!

1. Determine your yardage per curtain panel (as calculated in the Working Chart to Record Your Length Measurements, page 63) (A).

2. Determine the pattern's vertical repeat distance as described on page 66 (B).

3. Divide the yardage per curtain panel (A) by the vertical repeat distance (B).

4. Round this result up to the next whole number (C).

5. Multiply this number (C) by the vertical repeat distance (B) to determine the actual yardage required for each curtain panel so that pattern repeats will match top to bottom.

(continued on next page)

Here's an example for determining yardage per curtain panel with a pattern repeat:

1. Yardage per curtain panel (A) = 48".

2. Vertical repeat distance (B) = 18".

3. 48" ÷ 18" = 2.6667.

4. Round 2.667 up to 3 (C).

5. Therefore, 3 × 18" = 54", which is the actual yardage required per curtain panel (note that this is 6" longer than the original yardage per curtain panel you calculated).

Take the time to check and double-check your numbers *before* cutting your fabric. You will end up with some extra fabric to accommodate pattern matching, but depending on your creativity, this could be used in other interesting ways, such as tiebacks (see page 115), accent pillows, or even to add to your fabric stash and save for a later date. Keep in mind that large motifs with larger repeats will require purchasing more extra fabric.

Depending on where you are shopping, and the patience and helpfulness of the store attendant, you may request that your fabric be cut into the appropriate curtain panel lengths in the store. Sometimes this is helpful when you have limited work space at home.

JOINING FABRIC WIDTHS

If more than one fabric width is required to create each curtain panel (for example, if one width of fabric will not be wide enough for one panel and you need to piece two fabric widths together), you will want to match the pattern motifs along the joining seam so that the panels appear to be seamless. This pattern matching should be the first sewing you do when making the curtain panels.

If two full widths of fabric are required for each panel, it is advisable to cut one fabric width vertically in half and add each half width to the sides of a full width. This will prevent a seam in the center of your curtain panel and make the piecing less obvious. Similarly, if you are piecing together a partial width and a full width of fabric, the smaller width should be placed on the outside edge of the curtain (see illustration on page 64). This will also help hide the seam, making it less obvious.

Follow these simple steps to piece your panels together:

1. Lay one cut length of fabric, right side up, on your work surface. Note the motifs that repeat vertically along the outside edge of the fabric.

2. Locate where the same motifs repeat vertically along the edge of a second cut length of fabric. Using your iron, press a slight crease (folding the fabric with wrong sides together) down the length of fabric along this repeat line. The pressed edge will be used as seam allowance when stitching the panels together.

(continued on next page)

3. With both right sides facing up, position the pressed edge of the second fabric along the first fabric, carefully matching the pattern motifs.

4. Without disturbing the fabric placement, carefully unfold the second fabric so that both fabrics are now right sides together. Pin the layers together along the pressed seam allowance edge.

5. Use your sewing machine to stitch the panels together, on the wrong side of the fabric, in the ditch of the pressed crease.

6. Finish the seam allowances as desired (see Seam Variations on page 76). Press the panels open and marvel at your virtually invisible seam!

CHAPTER SIX

A FEW BASIC TECHNIQUES

Now that all the logistics (such as hanging hardware and styling details) are out of the way, there are just a few more details to cover. Before you get to the fun part of sewing, review the following tried and true techniques that you will want to have under your belt before making your curtains. From seam finishing techniques, to adding lining and curtain weights, these skills will come in handy when making nearly every curtain style.

FINISHING EDGES

REGARDLESS OF THE STYLE of curtain you plan to make, the very first thing you will need to do is press and straighten the fabric, squaring it up on all four sides. Technically, thanks to the beauty of weaving machinery, both selvages (the finished edges) will be parallel to one another, leaving the cut ends (the crosswise grain) as your only concern for squaring up. This can be accomplished using a couple different techniques:

- Pull a thread across the crosswise grain of the fabric and cut along this pulled thread.
- Use an L-shaped ruler, placed along the selvage edge of the fabric, to help square up and trim off the cut ends of the fabric.

Once the cut ends have been straightened, you should also trim off the selvage edges. The selvages are woven at a different tension than the main body of the fabric, and, if you leave them in place when making your curtains, you will likely end up with puckering along the sides of your curtain panels, leaving you with less-than-favorable results.

Double-fold Hems

This is a hem that has been folded and pressed twice to the wrong side of the fabric before being stitched in place. The fold depths vary, depending on either the type of fabric you are working with or the hem detail you are trying to achieve. Hemmed edges along the sides (for unlined curtains) are typically ½" wide, much narrower than bottom hems.

For bottom hems, as previously noted, standard hem depth is typically 2". For medium- to heavyweight fabric, you would first fold under your fabric ½" to the wrong side, then fold under an additional 2". For lighter-weight fabrics, such as linens or voiles, you would want a deeper double-fold hem so that the first folded edge does not show through the fabric. If following the 2" hem standard, you would first fold your fabric 2" to the wrong side, then an additional 2". Feel free to make adjustments to hem sizes as you see fit.

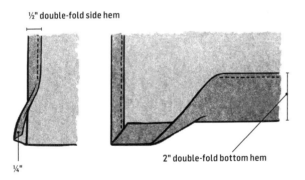

½" double-fold side hem

¼"

2" double-fold bottom hem

Mitering Hemmed Corners

This is a great technique to use in the hemmed bottom corners of your curtains. It is the only way you will achieve neat and tidy corners while reducing fabric bulk. Simply follow these easy steps:

1. Fold and press the double-fold hem allowances along the side and bottom edges of the curtain to the wrong side of the fabric. Do not stitch in place.

2. With the wrong side of the curtain facing up, unfold these edges near the corners; your pressed lines will still be visible. Make a diagonal fold in the corner of the fabric, matching up the lines at the intersection of the two innermost pressed lines. Press this diagonal fold in place.

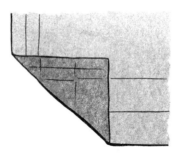

3. Refold the side and bottom hems in place along the original fold lines (keeping the diagonal fold from the previous step) and note how the side and bottom edges now miter together perfectly.

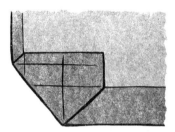

4. Stitch the side and bottom hems in place by hand or machine, as desired. You also may choose to invisibly slipstitch the mitered diagonal for added stability.

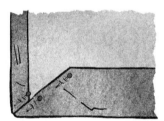

SEAM VARIATIONS

These techniques are useful when joining more than one width of fabric together in a curtain panel. The technique you use is really a matter of personal preference.

Basic Seam

This is the standard seam used to machine-stitch two pieces of fabric with right sides together. Because the edges of the seam allowance are unfinished, the basic seam is best suited for lined curtains, when this seam will be concealed. Otherwise, if your curtains are unlined, you may also choose to finish the raw edges of the seam allowance with a serger or zigzag stitch.

French Seam

This seam will completely hide raw edges and looks great from the wrong side of the fabric, so it is perfect for unlined curtains.

FRENCH SEAM

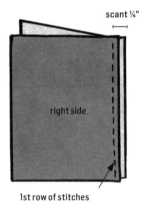

scant ¼"

right side

1st row of stitches

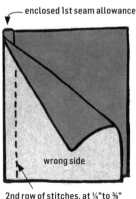

enclosed 1st seam allowance

wrong side

2nd row of stitches, at ¼" to ⅜"

Align the raw edges of two fabrics with wrong sides together and stitch with a scant ¼" seam. Turn the fabrics wrong side out, so that right sides are now together, and stitch another ¼" to ⅜" seam along the same edge, enclosing the raw edges. Press the seam to one side.

Flat Felled Seam

Like the French seam, this seam will also completely hide raw edges; the downside is that a line of stitching will be visible on the right side of your curtain panel. This may or may not be of any concern, depending on your preference. Position fabrics with right sides together and stitch along the raw edges at a ½" seam allowance. Trim one layer of this seam allowance to a scant ¼". Fold and press the wider seam allowance in half, encasing the trimmed allowance so that the raw edge is covered. Edgestitch the folded allowance to the fabric, close to the folded edge.

FLAT FELLED SEAM

Slip Stitch

This is a great basic invisible hand-sewing technique that you will find yourself using again and again, especially when you are working to achieve an invisible hem. It joins two fabric edges together in a variety of ways:

- If joining two folded edges, as in the case of mitered corners (see page 74), bring the needle out of one folded fabric edge, pierce the other folded edge, and run the needle ¼" under the fold. Bring the needle out and repeat this even ¼" stitch until both folded edges are joined.

- If joining a folded edge to a flat surface, such as the case with a bottom hem, pierce the folded edge of the hem and run the needle approximately ½" under the fold. Bring the needle out of the fold and pick up two threads from the main fabric. Continue alternating the needle between the folded edge and flat fabric until the entire edge has been hemmed. The only caution is that the thread should not be drawn too tightly; otherwise the hem will pucker and be visible from the right side of the curtain.

slip stitch along a mitered corner

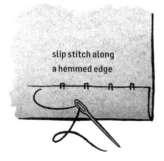

slip stitch along a hemmed edge

USING CURTAIN WEIGHTS

WEIGHTS ARE TRADITIONALLY ADDED to full-length curtains that are made of heavier fabrics. The primary purpose of the weights is to help curtains hang better. They are by no means mandatory, but you may find that they help give a more professional look to your finished curtains. Two weights are used per curtain panel, and they are hand-sewn into the folds of the curtain hem. Choose a size and weight that is appropriate to your curtain length, hem height, and fabric choice (you can often find a variety of options available at your local fabric retailer — sometimes you may find that a metal washer from your local hardware store will even do the trick).

For each weight, cut two squares of muslin fabric approximately 1" larger than the diameter of the weight. Place the two squares of muslin together and stitch along three sides at a $\frac{3}{8}$" to $\frac{1}{2}$" seam allowance. Insert a weight into the opening and stitch (by hand or machine) along the remaining open side to encase the weight. The covered weight is then slipped into each bottom corner of a curtain hem and invisibly hand-stitched in place. If mitering your corners, the weights would be inserted in step 3 of Mitering Hemmed Corners on page 74.

ADDING LINING

THERE ARE A FEW DIFFERENT ways to add lining to your curtains. The option you choose will depend on the look you are trying to achieve (for example, if you would like the lining to be somewhat visible on the right side of the curtain). Ultimately, use your personal preference and comfort level to determine your preferred lining construction.

None of the four options detailed below are terribly difficult. In all cases, linings are cut a minimum of ½" to 1" shorter than the curtain panel, and the hemmed bottom edge of the lining is placed a minimum of ½" to 1" above the hemmed bottom edge of the main curtain fabric. For all lined curtains, bottom edges of the lining and the curtain are hemmed separately, allowing the two fabrics to hang freely from one another. This will help prevent the appearance of bubbling and buckling in your finished lined curtains.

OPTION 1

Cut the lining the same width as your curtain panel and hem the bottom edges of the curtain and lining separately. Then sew the two panels together along the side edges, with *right* sides together. Turn the panels right side out and press. Next, construct the heading with both fabric layers treated as one. This is the simplest technique for lining curtains and requires the fewest calculations, but it may not be the look you are trying to achieve. Because the lining and the curtain fabric are cut to the same width, the lining will often peek out along the edges of the curtain, especially when the curtains are drawn open. If you have a contrasting lining that you want to showcase, this is the technique you should use, but otherwise consider one of the three remaining options.

OPTION 2

Again, cut the lining the same width as your curtain panel and hem both separately along the bottom edges. Then place the panels *wrong* sides together with side and top edges aligned. Press and stitch a double-fold hem along both side edges of the fabric, handling the two layers together as one fabric. As with the previous lining option, construct the heading with both fabric layers treated as one. This construction is great for shorter-length curtains (such as sill length, café, or valances); it might be a bit more challenging to wrangle longer lengths to lie smoothly. For those longer-length curtains, I suggest the following option.

OPTION 3

Cut the lining panel to the width you calculated for your finished curtain panel, but cut the actual curtain panel 4" wider than calculated finished width. As usual, hem the bottom edges of both panels separately. Pin both panels with the *right* sides together along the side edges and stitch them. Turn right side out; notice how the narrower lining panel causes the side edges of the main curtain fabric to turn to the lining side, creating a "facing" that hides the lining seam. Center the lining so that the facings along the side edges are equal and even; press. Again, construct the heading with both fabric layers treated as one.

OPTION 4

Similar to the previous option, cut the lining panel slightly narrower (approximately 1" to 2") than the width of your main curtain panel. This technique differs significantly in that you now hem both panels separately along both the side *and* bottom edges. Place these hemmed panels with *wrong* sides together and top edges aligned, and center the lining on the main curtain fabric. Hand-tack the loose lining in place along the side edges at even intervals, such as every 1". This will ensure that both layers handle as one. It will also prevent puckering so that the main curtain and the lining will hang smoothly and freely. Baste the two panels together along the top edge and construct the heading with both fabric layers treated as one. This lining option is probably the most labor intensive and time consuming of the four due to all the extra hemming and hand stitching.

CHAPTER SEVEN

SEWING YOUR CURTAINS

Now that you are well versed in the ins and outs of curtains — from rods, to headings, to hems, and everything in between — it's time to ready, set, sew! You will want to make sure you have a large, clean work space to lay out all your fabrics, which in turn will make the process go more smoothly. You may just find that your dining room table is the best option. Once you get to work making your curtain panels, concentrate on the pressing, lining, and heading details to give your curtains a professional look with just the right amount of flare to liven up your living space.

All of the projects in this book are intended as guidelines for you to create the perfect custom curtains to personalize your living space. With that in mind, length and width measurements are not given. For each project, choose any length you like, as short as valance and as long as puddle, or any variation in between. You will measure your window and curtain rod to input the appropriate measurements into each project. The end result will be the perfect curtains for your space.

Specific supplies are listed with each project, but there are some basic sewing items you'll need when making every type of curtain. Here's a short list of what to have on hand:

- sewing machine and needles
- sharp fabric-cutting scissors
- straight pins
- tape measure and yardstick
- hand-sewing needles
- iron and ironing board

Before starting any of the following curtain projects, you should have already finalized the decisions listed below regarding your curtains:

- inside-mount versus outside-mount
- hardware choice and placement
- window measurements
- curtain length and desired fullness
- curtain heading style
- lined versus unlined
- number of curtain panels you plan to make

UNLINED ROD POCKET CURTAINS

With or without a ruffled header, this curtain style is about as basic as it comes, and basic is definitely not a bad thing. It's probably the easiest curtain for beginners, and it can help you develop a true understanding for taking measurements and translating those numbers into real, functional curtain panels. Make the style a little more relaxed and practical by adding a wider rod pocket along the top edge. You will find these curtains, long or short, to be a great staple in many rooms in your home and will no doubt come back to this style again and again.

rod pocket casing

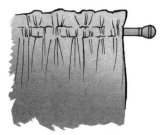

rod pocket casing with header

REQUIRED MATERIALS
- Curtain fabric
- Thread
- Weights (optional)

(continued on next page)

ESTIMATE YARDAGE

1. Measure your window to determine the desired finished width and length of your curtains (see Taking Accurate Measurements page 47).

2. Determine your desired fullness, and from there, how much fabric you will need per curtain panel (see chapter 5). Add the necessary allowances for all hemmed edges, as well as a header, if you choose to add one. Also include any additional length to match pattern repeats (see Matching Pattern Repeats on page 65), if necessary.

Header Tip

Remember, additional yardage is required for a header, if you choose to add one above the rod pocket. If so, determine how tall you'd like your header to be and multiply this number by 2. Add this additional amount to the total length before cutting your curtain panels.

MAKE THE CURTAIN PANELS

1. Cut, press, and square (see page 72) the required number of curtain panels.

2. Using your preferred technique, seam the fabric widths together (see page 76), if necessary, to create the appropriate width for each curtain panel (see Joining Fabric Widths on pages 69–70).

3. Press under a ½" double-fold hem along both of the side edges of the curtain panels. Pin and stitch the side hems in place, using your preferred technique.

4. Press under the bottom edge of each curtain panel ½" to the wrong side. Then press under an additional 2" to create a double-fold hem. If these are full-length curtains, you may also choose to add curtain weights before stitching the hem in place (see Using Curtain Weights on page 79).

5. Press under the top raw edge of each curtain panel ½" to the wrong side. Then press under an additional amount equal to one-half the curtain rod circumference plus at least ½" to create the rod pocket casing. Pin and stitch this casing in place close to the folded edge. Read on if you have chosen to add a header.

If you have chosen to add a header, complete step 5 as follows: Press under the top raw edge of each curtain panel ½" to the wrong side. Then press under an additional amount equal to one-half the curtain rod circumference plus at least ½" *plus*

Adding a Return

If you choose to add a return to your rod pocket curtains, you would do so in step 5, before stitching the casing in place. Press the casing as indicated and follow the instructions on pages 90–91 for Creating a Return Allowance.

(continued on next page)

half of the header height. Pin and stitch the header in place. If the header depth is wider than the seam allowance guidelines on your sewing machine, you may stick a piece of masking tape on your machine to use as a stitching guide. Stitch the rod pocket casing in place close to the second folded edge.

FOLDING THE ROD POCKET CASING AND HEADER

half the header height

half the rod pocket casing height plus ½"

½" turned to the wrong side

stitching line for header

stitching line for casing

Need a Lining?

Follow the instructions for Lined Rod Pocket Curtains (on page 92) to add lining to any of the projects in this chapter. Or choose one of the four options on page 80 for variations on adding a lining.

Calculating Casing Height

If you didn't calculate up front the exact casing height for your curtain panels, you will need to work backward a bit to stitch the rod pocket in place. First, from the bottom hemmed edge of your curtain panel, measure up the desired finished length of the curtains and mark this point with a pin. Press under the top edge of the fabric to the wrong side at this pin mark and press. Determine your desired casing height plus at least 1" and trim off any additional fabric from this unfinished edge. Turn the raw edge ½" to the wrong side and stitch the casing in place close to this folded edge.

FOLDING THE ROD POCKET CASING

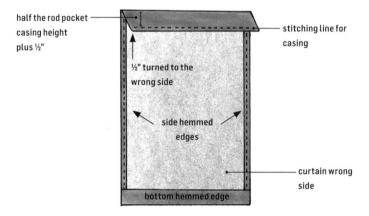

half the rod pocket casing height plus ½"

stitching line for casing

½" turned to the wrong side

side hemmed edges

curtain wrong side

bottom hemmed edge

Creating a Return Allowance for Straight Rods

1. Before stitching the heading in place, unfold the upper edge of the pressed heading.

2. On the right side of the curtain panel, measure and mark the return distance (the distance from the center of the rod to the wall) on both finished side edges of the curtain panel.

3. At these marks, stitch a vertical buttonhole slightly shorter than the height of the rod pocket casing, taking care that this

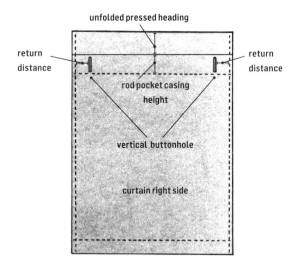

unfolded pressed heading

return distance

return distance

rod pocket casing height

vertical buttonhole

curtain right side

buttonhole does not extend beyond the casing height (or into the header, if adding). You may also fuse a piece of heavyweight interfacing to the wrong side of the curtain at each buttonhole placement, prior to stitching the buttonholes, for reinforcement.

4. Refold along the original pressed lines and begin stitching the heading (and header, if adding) in place per the instructions on pages 87–88. When this technique is used, the ends of the curtain rod will exit the curtain through the buttonholes (not through the actual ends of the rod pocket casing).

5. When the finished curtain is hung on the rod, the return can now extend to the wall, providing extra privacy. The return is typically secured to the wall with the use of a hook and eyelet, such as those used for curtain tiebacks.

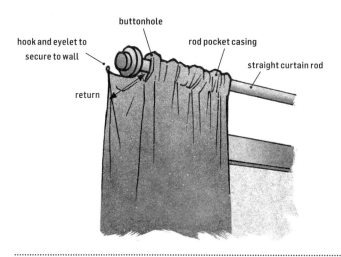

buttonhole

hook and eyelet to
secure to wall

rod pocket casing

straight curtain rod

return

LINED ROD POCKET CURTAINS

Again, with or without a ruffled header, this is a great classic style, but take it a step further by adding lining. Once you work through this lined curtain project, you should feel confident enough to line any curtains you make!

REQUIRED MATERIALS

- Curtain fabric
- Lining fabric
- Thread
- Weights (optional)

ESTIMATE YARDAGE

1. Measure your window to determine the desired finished width and length of your curtains (see Taking Accurate Measurements on page 47).

2. Determine your desired fullness, and from there, how much fabric and lining you will need per curtain panel (see chapter 5). Add the necessary allowances for all hemmed edges, as well as a header, if you choose to add one. Also include any additional length to match pattern repeats (see Matching Pattern Repeats on page 65), if necessary.

Lining Tip

You may also choose to review Adding Lining in Chapter 6 on page 80 to review three additional techniques on how to line your curtains.

Header Tip

Remember, additional yardage is required for a header, if you choose to add one above the rod pocket. If so, determine how tall you'd like your header to be and multiply this number by 2. Add this additional amount to the total length before cutting your curtain panels.

MAKE THE LINED CURTAIN PANELS

1. Cut, press, and square (see page 72) the required number of curtain and lining panels. The lining panels should be cut the same width and 1½" shorter than the main curtain fabric.

2. Using your preferred technique, seam fabric widths together (see page 76), if necessary, to create the appropriate width for each curtain and lining panel (see Joining Fabric Widths on pages 69–70).

3. Press under the bottom edge of each curtain panel ½" to the wrong side. Then press under an additional 2" to create a double-fold hem. Pin and stitch this bottom hem in place. If these are full-length curtains, you may also choose to add curtain weights (see Curtain Weights on page 79). Repeat to hem the bottom edge of each lining panel, omitting the weights.

(continued on next page)

4. Place a curtain and lining panel with wrong sides together, aligning the side and top edges (the bottom edge of the lining should be 1½" shorter than the main curtain fabric). Handle the two fabrics as one and press under a ½" double-fold hem along both side edges of the curtain panels. Pin and stitch the side hems in place.

5. Again, handling the two fabrics as one, press under the top edge of your curtain panel ½" to the wrong side. Then press under an amount equal to one-half the curtain rod circumference plus at least ½" to create the rod pocket casing. Pin and stitch this casing in place close to the folded edge.

Return Tip

If you choose to add a return allowance to your lined curtain, see the tips and instructions on pages 87–91.

TAB TOP AND TIE TOP CURTAINS

These curtain styles are more relaxed and informal than a rod pocket style. The top edge of the curtain is defined by a row of fabric loops or ties, placed at regular intervals, which help showcase your curtain rod. You may choose to add a bit of flair by making contrasting fabric loops or ties or even adding decorative buttons to your loops. For tie top curtains, experiment with different tying techniques (knots or bows) to change up the look and feel of these curtains. Do keep in mind that frequent opening and closing of this curtain type may put excess strain on the individual tabs and ties, in which case you may choose to space them at closer intervals to provide additional support. The main instructions are the same for both curtain styles, with options given for tabs or ties.

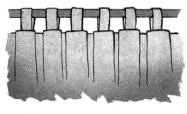

tab top curtains

tie top curtains

(continued on next page)

REQUIRED MATERIALS

- Curtain fabric
- Thread
- Weights (optional)

ESTIMATE YARDAGE

1. Measure your window to determine the desired finished width and length of your curtains (see Taking Accurate Measurements on page 47).

2. Determine your desired fullness, and from there, how much fabric you will need per curtain panel (see chapter 5). Add the necessary allowances for all hemmed edges. Note that the tabs or ties will take the place of the heading allowance, so you need not add a heading allowance to your calculations, however, you will need extra fabric for a facing (see step 3). If you plan to use the main curtain fabric for making the tabs or ties, refer to step 4 to add any additional yardage for making them. Also be sure to include any additional length to match pattern repeats (see Matching Pattern Repeats on page 65), if necessary.

3. You will also require an additional facing piece for the top edge of your curtain to conceal the raw edges of the tabs and ties. Cut the facing piece the same width you cut your curtain panel (less 1") by 4" long. (Note that if you have to piece curtain panel widths together, you will also

need to piece your facing widths together.) Again, be sure to add the appropriate extra fabric for the facing to your yardage requirements in step 2.

FOR TABS OR TIES

4. **For Tabs (if appropriate):** Calculate the necessary number of tabs required for your curtain width, spacing them approximately 4" apart. To do so, divide the finished curtain panel width by 4. Round the number down to determine the total number of tabs required, and add one extra tab. The individual curtain tabs should be cut 5" wide x 9" long each. (The finished circumference of the tabs will be 8", which should move easily over any curtain rod you are using; otherwise, you may choose to adjust the tab length accordingly.) Be sure to add the appropriate extra fabric for the tabs to your yardage requirements in step 2.

   For Ties (if appropriate): Calculate the necessary number of ties required for your curtain width, spacing them approximately 6" apart. To do so, divide the finished curtain panel width by 6. Round the number down to determine the number of ties, and add one extra tie. The individual curtain ties should be cut 4" wide × 26" long each. (The finished width of the ties will be 1"; they will be folded in half lengthwise, so the two ties that tie together will each be 12" long.) Be sure to add the appropriate extra fabric for the ties to your yardage requirements in step 2.

(continued on next page)

MAKE THE CURTAIN PANELS

1. Cut, press, and square (see page 72) the required number of curtain panels.

2. Using your preferred technique, seam fabric widths together (see page 76), if necessary, to create the appropriate width for your curtain panel (see Joining Fabric Widths on pages 69–70). If necessary, repeat to piece together widths for the facing piece.

3. Press under a ½" double-fold hem along both of the side edges of the curtain panels. Pin and stitch the hems in place.

4. Press under the bottom edge of each curtain panel ½" to the wrong side. Then press under an additional 2" to create a double-fold hem. Pin and stitch this bottom hem in place. If these are full-length curtains, you may also choose to add curtain weights (see Curtain Weights on page 79).

MAKING TABS (IF APPROPRIATE)

5. Fold each tab piece in half lengthwise, with right sides together, aligning the long edges. Stitch the long raw edge at a ½" seam allowance. Turn the tab pieces right side out so that the seam runs along the center of one side and press flat.

6. Fold each tab in half, aligning the short raw ends so the seam is on the inside of the folded tab. Place the first and last tabs along the top raw edge of the curtain panel, approximately ½" away from the hemmed side edges, aligning raw

edges. Evenly space the remaining tabs in between the two end tabs, again aligning raw edges. Pin the tabs in place, and stitch to secure them at a ¼" seam allowance.

ATTACHING THE FOLDED TABS AND FACING TO THE CURTAIN

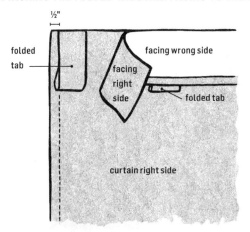

MAKING TIES (IF APPROPRIATE)

5. Fold a tie piece in half lengthwise, with wrong sides together, aligning the raw edges, and press a center crease. Open the strip and fold and press both short ends ½" to the wrong side. Fold and press the long raw edges on both sides of the tie into the center crease. Refold along the original fold line, aligning the pressed edges on three sides, and press. Edgestitch along the three pressed edges of the tie (both short ends and one long edge) to close. Repeat to make the remaining tie pieces.

(continued on next page)

6. Fold each tie in half, aligning the short finished ends, and press at the fold to mark the center. Place the first and last folded ties on the right side of the curtain panel, along the raw top edge, approximately 1" away from the hemmed side edges. The folded center of the ties should align with the raw top edge of the curtain. Evenly space the remaining ties in between the two end ties, again aligning the folded centers of the ties with the raw top edge of the curtain. Pin the ties in place and stitch to secure them with a ¼" seam allowance.

ATTACHING THE FOLDED TIES AND FACING TO THE CURTAIN

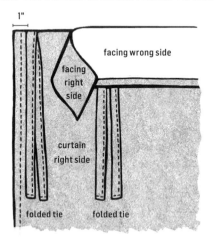

Making Ribbon Ties

As an alternate to using fabric for your ties, you can also use ribbon, such as grosgrain or velvet, or twill tape. Choose a ribbon or twill tape that is approximately 1" wide. Once you determine how many ties you will need per curtain panel, multiply this number by 26". Divide the total number by 36" to get your ribbon yardage requirement. Simply skip step 5, on page 99, and substitute the 26" cut pieces of ribbon in place of the ties in step 6. Finish the ends of the ties using your preferred technique (burning, hemming, or cutting at an angle).

FINISHING THE CURTAINS

7. Press under the side and bottom edges of the facing piece ½" to the wrong side. With right sides together, position the facing on the curtain panel, aligning the raw top edges and the folded side edges. The tabs or ties will be sandwiched in between the layers.

8. Stitch the facing and curtain panel together along the top raw edge at a ½" seam allowance. Turn the facing to the wrong side of the curtain and press. Edgestitch (or slip-stitch, if desired) the facing and curtain together along the folded side edges and along the long folded edge of the facing.

9. Repeat to complete any additional tab or tie top curtain panels.

HIDDEN TAB CURTAINS

This cross between rod pocket and tab top curtains offers a somewhat cleaner, more sophisticated look than rod pocket and a less casual look than exposed tab top curtains. When drawn open, the top edge of the curtain falls into dramatic folds, giving the illusion of pleats not unlike traditional drapery. When closed, the hidden tabs create subtle, soft, even pleats. It's a great choice for most rooms in your home, perhaps best suited to longer-length curtains. If you are looking for an opportunity to add more visual interest, try adding a wide contrast border along the bottom edge of your curtain panels. Optional instructions are given for this border, which you could easily use with any curtain project in this book. As an aside, adding a contrast border is also a great way to lengthen curtain panels that are too short.

REQUIRED MATERIALS

- Curtain fabric, with optional contrasting fabric for the border, if desired
- Basic white or natural quilter's-weight cotton for hidden tabs
- Thread
- Weights (optional)

ESTIMATE YARDAGE

1. Measure your window to determine the desired finished width and length of your curtains (see Taking Accurate Measurements on page 47).

2. Determine your desired fullness and, from there, how much fabric you will need per curtain panel (see chapter 5), adding the necessary allowances for all hemmed

(continued on next page)

Calculate an Optional Contrast Border

First decide on the finished length of the border. Once you have that, you can calculate the new main panel length. To do so, take your original main panel length, subtract the contrast border finished length and bottom hem allowance, and add ½" seam allowance. For the contrast border length, take the desired finished border length, add bottom hem allowance and ½" seam allowance. (If you are using a printed fabric, you may also require additional length to match pattern repeats).

edges, plus 5½" for the hem allowance at the top edge of
the curtain. Note that the curtain rod will thread through
the hidden tabs on the back of the curtain and that the
top edge of the curtain will sit 1" above the rod. Be sure
to also include any additional length to match pattern
repeats (see Matching Pattern Repeats on page 65),
if necessary.

3. Calculate the necessary number of hidden tabs required
    for each panel width, spacing them approximately 7"
    apart. To do so, divide the finished curtain panel width
    by 7. Round the number down to determine the number
    of tabs, and add one extra tab. The individual curtain tabs
    should be cut 5" wide x 5" long each from the quilter's-
    weight cotton. (These tabs will easily accommodate a
    curtain rod up to 1¼" in diameter or 4" circumference.)

MAKE THE CURTAIN PANELS

1. Cut, press, and square (see page 72) the required number
    of curtain panels.

2. Using your preferred technique, seam fabric widths
    together (see page 76), if necessary, to create the appro-
    priate width for each curtain panel (see Joining Fabric
    Widths on pages 69–70).

Add the Optional Contrast Border

If you intend to add a contrast border, now would be the time to add it to your main curtain panel fabric. If necessary, piece the border widths together as described in step 2. Once the widths are pieced together, stitch the border to the main fabric using a ½" seam allowance together with either a French or flat felled seam (see page 76). Proceed with the remainder of the instructions as written.

3. Press under a ½" double-fold hem along both side edges of the curtain panels. Pin and stitch the hems in place.

4. Press under the bottom edge of each curtain panel ½" to the wrong side. Then press under an additional 2" to create a double-fold hem. Pin and stitch this bottom hem in place. If these are full-length curtains, you may also choose to add curtain weights (see Curtain Weights on page 79).

5. Fold each tab piece in half lengthwise, with right sides together, aligning the lengthwise edges. Stitch along this raw edge at a ½" seam allowance. Turn the tab pieces right side out so that the seam runs along the center of one side (this is now the wrong side) and press flat. Press under both unfinished ends of each tab ½" to wrong side (the side with the seam).

(continued on next page)

6. Press under the raw top edge of your curtain panel ½" to the wrong side. Then press under the top edge 5" to the wrong side. Do not stitch in place.

7. On the wrong side of the curtain panel, place the first and last tabs seam side up along the bottom folded edge of the hem, approximately 1" away from the side hemmed edges. The bottom folded ½" end of the tabs should tuck neatly underneath the folded edge of the hem. Evenly space the

ATTACHING THE HIDDEN TABS

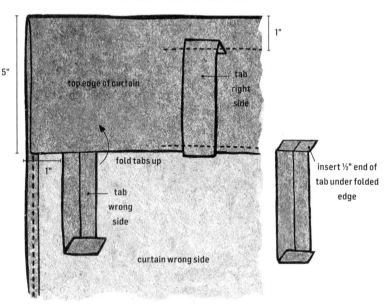

5"

1"

top edge of curtain

tab right side

fold tabs up

1"

tab wrong side

curtain wrong side

insert ½" end of tab under folded edge

remaining tabs in between the two ends tabs, again tucking the folded ends of the tabs under the fold of the hem. Pin the tabs in place and fold them up.

8. Pin and stitch the hem in place, close to the bottom folded edge, stitching down the bottom edges of the tabs at the same time. Stitch a 1" hem along the top folded edge of the curtain, catching and securing the tops of the tabs in the stitching line.

9. Repeat to complete any additional curtain panels.

GROMMET TOP CURTAINS

For this casual, modern curtain style, grommets are set along the top edge of the curtain panel, and the rod is inserted directly through each grommet. When drawn open, grommet top curtains give the illusion of wide pleats, as the curtain falls into nice, heavy folds. The fuller you make this curtain style, the more likely you are to also enjoy the pronounced folds when the curtains are drawn closed. You can find both metal and plastic grommets in a variety of sizes and finishes. This style also works well if you wish to create a custom shower curtain.

REQUIRED MATERIALS

- Curtain fabric
- Individual grommets, large enough to accommodate your curtain rod (the number required is calculated in step 3, pages 109–110), or see the Grommet Size Tip on page 110 for smaller grommets
- A strip of heavyweight fusible interfacing to reinforce the grommets
- Thread
- Weights (optional)
- Tools for installing grommets, as needed per manufacturer's instructions

Buttonholes: An Alternate to Grommets

If you don't like the look of grommet hardware but you like how this curtain hangs, simply omit the grommets and replace them with vertical buttonholes. Just remember that the buttonhole openings need to accommodate your curtain rod plus about ½" for ease. This larger opening will help prevent unnecessary wear on the buttonholes as a result of opening and closing the curtain.

ESTIMATE YARDAGE

1. Measure your window to determine the desired finished width and length of your curtains (see Taking Accurate Measurements on page 47).

2. Determine your desired fullness, and from there, how much fabric you will need per curtain panel (see chapter 5), adding the necessary allowances for all hemmed edges. The top of the curtain rod will be even with the top of the grommet hole, and the top edge of the actual curtain will sit 1" above the rod. The top hem allowance should be the diameter of the grommet plus 2½". Be sure to also include any additional length to match pattern repeats (see Matching Pattern Repeats on page 65), if necessary.

3. Calculate the necessary number of grommets required for each curtain panel, spacing them approximately 5" apart.

(continued on next page)

To do so, divide the finished curtain panel width by 5. Round the number down to the next whole number and add one extra grommet. You *must have an even number of grommets per curtain panel* so that both the leading and the return edges of the curtain will fold toward the wall, so be sure to adjust your total grommets required to an even number, if necessary.

4. You will also require a strip of interfacing for the top edge of your curtain to reinforce the grommets. Cut the fusible interfacing piece the same width as your curtain panel by the diameter of the grommet plus 2½".

Grommet Size Tip

Although this project calls for large grommets to accommodate the curtain rod, it is also possible to complete this project with smaller grommets that would hang from the rod with the use of curtain rings or hooks. Keep in mind that the top edge of your curtain would be at the bottom of the rings/ hooks, so plan your finished curtain length accordingly. The closer your grommets are spaced together, the firmer and straighter the top edge of the curtain will be. Grommets spaced farther apart will result in a slouchier top edge. Both options are fine; it just depends on your personal preference.

MAKE THE CURTAIN PANELS

1. Cut, press, and square (see page 72) the required number of curtain panels.

2. Using your preferred technique, seam fabric widths together (see page 76), if necessary, to create the appropriate width for your curtain panel (see Joining Fabric Widths on pages 69–70). Fuse the interfacing to the wrong side of your curtain panels along the top edge, following the manufacturer's instructions.

3. Press under a ½" double-fold hem along both side edges of the curtain panels. Pin and stitch the hems in place.

4. Press under the bottom edge of your curtain panel ½" to the wrong side. Then press under an additional 2" to create a double-fold hem. Pin and stitch this bottom hem in place. If these are full-length curtains, you may also choose to add curtain weights (see Curtain Weights on page 79).

5. Press under the raw top edge of your curtain panel ½" to the wrong side. Then press under the top edge by the diameter of the grommet plus 2" to the wrong side. Pin and stitch the hem in place, close to the folded edge.

(continued on next page)

6. On the right side of the curtain, mark the placement of the first and last grommets along the top edge of the curtain panel, centered top to bottom in the stitched hem, approximately 1" in from the hemmed side edges. Evenly space the remaining grommets in between the two end grommets, and mark placements. *Double-check that you have an even number of grommets per curtain panel.*

7. Insert the grommets following the manufacturer's instructions.

8. Repeat to complete any additional grommet top curtain panels.

Optional Buttonholes

If you choose to add vertical buttonholes in place of grommets, do so in step 6, substituting buttonholes for grommets.

INSTANT NO-SEW CURTAINS

Curtains don't get much easier than this! Perhaps you're pressed for time, not confident in your sewing ability, or you already have the perfect ready-made, hemmed item (such as a tablecloth, bedsheet, or even tea towels for café curtains) to use that will easily transform into the window covering of your dreams. With the help of some curtain clips to hold the hemmed item in place, get ready for the fastest curtains ever.

REQUIRED MATERIALS

- Hemmed, ready-made items to use for curtains
- Curtain clips
- Iron-on hem tape (optional)

PREPARE FOR INSTALLATION

Measure your ready-made item and window to determine exactly how you'd like the item to hang (see Taking Accurate Measurements on page 47). Keep in mind that the top edge of your curtain would be at the bottom of the clips, so plan your finished curtain length accordingly.

If your ready-made item is too long and you prefer not to shorten it, you can create a cuffed curtain by folding over the top edge of the fabric to the right side, and clipping it in place along the fold line, creating a somewhat romantic appearance.

(continued on next page)

HANG THE CURTAIN PANELS

Decide how many clips you will need to hold the curtain in place. It may take some trial and error to achieve your desired look. In any case, keep in mind that the closer together the clips are spaced, the firmer and straighter the top edge of the curtain will be; placing the clips farther apart will result in a slouchier top edge. Both options are fine; it all depends on your personal preference. Just make sure that the clips are evenly spaced.

No-Sew Hemming Tip

If the dimensions of your pre-hemmed, ready-made item are not going to work well in your space (in either length, width, or both), you can shorten and finish the edges without the use of a sewing machine. Simply use iron-on hem tape to clean-finish your cut edges. Press under the cut edges of the fabric to the wrong side in the same width as the iron-on hem tape. Lay a strip of hem tape inside the folded edge and iron. The hem tape will fuse the fold in place, completely eliminating the need for a sewing machine!

FABRIC TIEBACKS

Fabric tiebacks are both decorative and functional, and may be straight, curved, welted, ruffled, and more. They are most helpful to hold full-length curtains open and out of the way. If you want your tieback to match your curtains, add the additional fabric needed to your curtain yardage requirements (or you may have enough extra fabric from matching pattern repeats). You will likely need to purchase additional hardware to secure your tieback to the wall. Instructions are given below for both a straight tieback as well as a curved one.

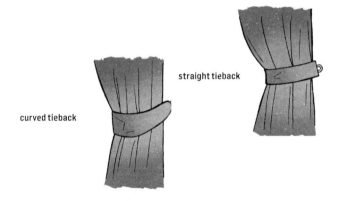

straight tieback

curved tieback

(continued on next page)

REQUIRED MATERIALS

- Tieback fabric
- Heavyweight fusible interfacing to reinforce the tieback
- Thread
- 2 metal or plastic tieback rings (approximately ½" to ¾") per tieback
- 1 tieback wall hook per tieback to secure
- Paper and pencil for drafting the curved tieback pattern (optional)

DETERMINE TIEBACK DIMENSIONS

1. A fabric tieback may range in length from 20" for a standard-size window to 36" for a very wide window. Standards aside, the best way to determine the appropriate length is to use a flexible tape measure and drape it around your curtain panel at the location that is most visually pleasing to you. Loosen or tighten your tape measure around the curtain until you are satisfied with the drape of the curtain when it is held back from the window. Make note of the length on the tape measure.

2. The height of the tieback is also a matter of personal preference. Generally speaking, keep your finished tieback in the 2"–6" range. If you're not sure what will look best, it's always possible to create a mock-up using paper or even extra fabric, if you have it on hand.

STRAIGHT TIEBACK

1. Once you have determined the desired finished tieback dimensions, cut the tieback from your fabric as follows: finished length plus 1" by twice the finished height plus 1". In addition, cut one piece of interfacing matching the finished dimensions of your tieback. For each curtain panel, cut one fabric tieback and one piece of interfacing.

2. Press under both short ends of the tieback ½" to the wrong side. Fold the tieback in half lengthwise, with right sides together, aligning the long edges. Stitch along the raw long edge at a ½" seam allowance. Turn right side out so that the seam runs along the center of one side (now the back side of the tieback) and press flat.

3. Insert the fusible interfacing inside the tieback, with the fusible side toward the seam side of the tieback. Fuse in place following manufacturer's instructions. Slipstitch the ends of the tieback closed.

4. Hand-stitch one ring on the seam side at each end of the tieback, centered on the seam, so that each one overhangs the edge slightly. At the desired location, install the wall hook so that it will be concealed when the curtain panel is both open and closed, or you may choose to leave it exposed if the hook is more decorative. Place one ring on

(continued on next page)

the hook, loop the tieback around the curtain panel, and place the second ring over the same hook.

STITCHING THE TIEBACK RINGS IN PLACE

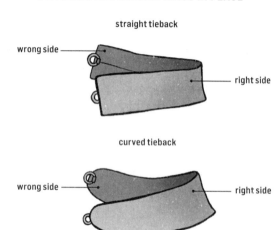

straight tieback

wrong side

right side

curved tieback

wrong side

right side

CURVED TIEBACK

1. For a curved tieback, you will want to draft a paper pattern in which the tieback is wider in the center and tapers at the ends, which gracefully slant upward. This is best done through trial and error. Sketch out a few tieback shapes at actual size, cut out the paper templates, and hold them up to your curtain to see what you like best. Once you've made a decision, add ½" seam allowance around the outside edge of your paper pattern.

2. For each tieback, use the paper pattern to cut two pieces from your main fabric and one piece from the fusible interfacing. Fuse the interfacing to the wrong side of one of the fabric pieces, following manufacturer's instructions.

3. Position an interfaced and non-interfaced tieback piece with right sides together, aligning the raw edges. Stitch together at a ½" seam allowance, leaving an opening along the bottom edge for turning. Notch the seam allowance around the curved edges, turn right side out, and press. Slipstitch the opening used for turning closed. If desired, you may also choose to edgestitch around the perimeter of the tieback. Follow step 4 on pages 117–118 for attaching the rings and wall hook.

Standard Metric Conversion Formulas

WHEN THE MEASUREMENT GIVEN IS	TO CONVERT IT TO	MULTIPLY IT BY
yards	meters (m)	0.9144
yards	centimeters (cm)	91.44
inches	centimeters (cm)	2.54
inches	millimeters (mm)	25.4
inches	meters (m)	0.0254

Standard Equivalents

U.S.	METRIC	U.S.	METRIC
⅛ inch	3.20 mm	⅝ inch	1.59 cm
¼ inch	6.35 mm	¾ inch	1.91 cm
⅜ inch	9.50 mm	⅞ inch	2.22 cm
½ inch	1.27 cm	1 inch	2.54 cm

INDEX

Page numbers in *italic* indicate illustrations; page numbers in **bold** indicate tables or charts.

OTHER STOREY BOOKS YOU WILL ENJOY

Fabric-by-Fabric One-Yard Wonders
by Rebecca Yaker and Patricia Hoskins

Enjoy this collection of 101 beautiful, stylish, and fun projects that use a diverse range of fabrics. Each project comes with step-by-step illustrated instructions and a complete cutting layout, and all required pattern pieces are included.
416 pages. Hardcover with concealed wire-o and patterns.
ISBN 978-1-60342-586-5.

How to Make Slipcovers by Patricia Hoskins

Give your furniture a new look with these step-by-step, illustrated instructions. This straightforward guide from Patricia Hoskins, co-author of the best-selling One-Yard Wonders series, will show you how to make custom-fit slipcovers for chairs, ottomans, sofas, and more.
128 pages. Paper. ISBN 978-1-61212-525-1.

Sew Up a Home Makeover by Lexie Barnes

Transform any space with these 50 fresh, fun sewing projects. Designer Lexie Barnes teaches you how easy and inexpensive it can be to personalize your home.
160 pages. Paper. ISBN 978-1-60342-797-5.

The Sewing Answer Book by Barbara Weiland Talbert

This friendly, reassuring resource will answer beginning and advanced sewing questions. The question-and-answer format makes it easy to quickly find what you need, for both hand and machine sewing.
432 pages. Flexibind with cloth spine. ISBN 978-1-60342-543-8.

Spruce: A Step-by-Step Guide to Upholstery and Design
by Amanda Brown

Customize your home with the help of this fully photographed course in the art of taking furniture down to its frame and restoring it with new upholstery. These projects will teach you all the skills you need to suit your own taste and style.
400 pages. Hardcover. ISBN 978-1-61212-137-6.